ONLY FOR HER

THE RISE AND FALL OF A RELATIONSHIP TOLD THROUGH POETRY

ANKIT ARYA

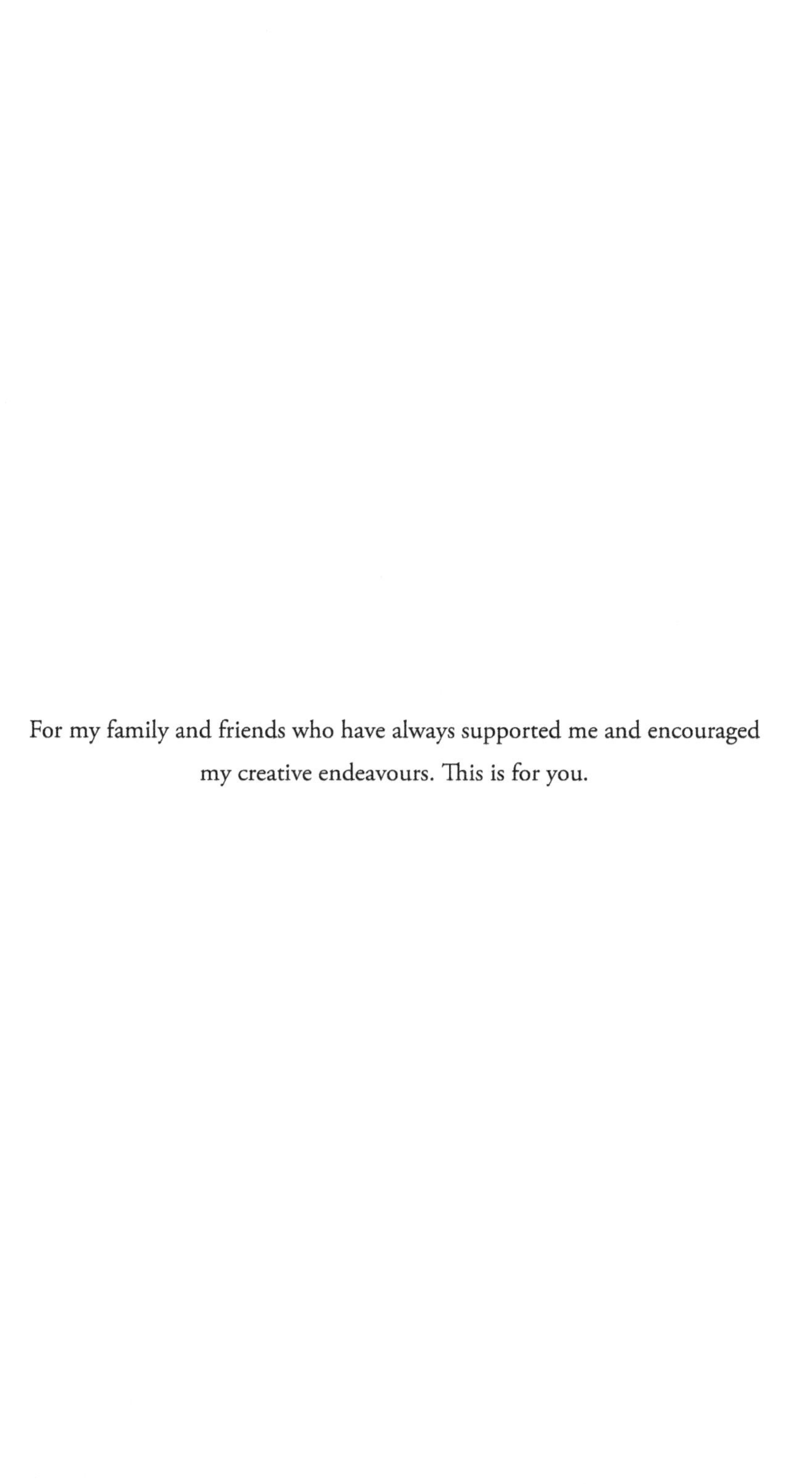

For my family and friends who have always supported me and encouraged my creative endeavours. This is for you.

Contents

Contents

Contents

Foreword

This is a collection of poems written about a former relationship. It was the first time I opened myself up to a person after many years. My emotions were always in a flux and writing helped me center my thought process. Dealing with depression and anxiety made everything more complicated. This collection chronicles the rise and fall of this relationship.

Preface

Ankit Arya was born in Delhi and has spent the last decade in Mumbai. He studied Journalism and Mass Communication in his undergrad and Film Making in post grad.

He is currently working in Film Production as a 1st Assistant Director. He hopes to direct his own stories soon.

Writing has been his passion for over two decades. He loves writing stories, screenplays and poems. He has since published his debut novel, "Mr Shadow and the Night of the Four Crimes".

Prologue

All poems in this collection are written from my perspective to my former lover. They either are about how I felt during that time in a relationship, me trying to understand her struggles and her daily life, memories I wanted to make with her, and retellings of the moments we had together.

1. I want you, I need you

I'd like to keep this short and sweet
Can't wait till the next time we meet
I look at you and the stars align
You make me special all of the time
Nothing can stop me from feeling this good
When you're around me I'm in a happy happy mood
Always just dancing to your favourite tunes
You make the happiest man, oh you do
I want you to stay
I need you everyday
I can't imagine life without you bae
I want you I need you in each and every way
Oh you got some sass
And a cute little ass
And I don't mean to be crass
Well I do maybe just a little, a little splash
You look at me and I lose my mind
Not loving you seems like a crime
I want you I need you all of the time
Oh won't you stay with me in a love so blind
I want you to stay
I need you everyday
I can't imagine life without you bae
I want you I need you in each and every way

You're all that I think of day in and out
I want you I need you is all I dream about
Be it in the day or in the dark dark night
There's something about you that's just so right
I'd be a fool to have second doubts
Sometimes I just need you to hold me down and shout
How you feel about me, it makes me feel so good
You make me special no matter what you do
I want you to stay
I need you everyday
I can't imagine life without you bae
I want you I need you in each and every way

2. The Goddess of NO!

She's picking my heart strings
One at a time
She's singing along
In an A B rhyme
She's made for idol worship
And I'm a believer
I'm a man of temptation
And god I need her
She gives one look
And I'm down on my knees
Let me pray to you
Oh goddess please
Hair of passion
And eyes of soul
Laughter so sexy
I feel whole
Lips so tender
They remove the gloom
The goddess shines
She's in bloom
Oh you make me feel like
The world is made for me and you
Days without worship
Are all agony

You bring the spice
And the harmony
I need a temple to us
Just you and me
Where I can worship
And we can be free
And I can lay down
The daily prayer
I'm sure you've heard it
It's all I hear
It goes…
Hair of passion
And eyes of soul
Laughter so sexy
I feel whole
Lips so tender
They remove the gloom
The goddess shines
She's in bloom
Oh you make me feel like
The world is made for me and you

3. Forever

One look at you
And my world stops spinning
Time is at a standstill
I know I am winning
Holding you close
Brings a smile to my face
It only leaves
When we part our ways
Everything seems special
With you by my side
This will last forever
Till the end of time
But they say nothing lasts forever
And I know they're just wrong
They don't know our love
Is timeless like a song
I love you forever
Forever and more
I'll stand by your side
Through all your ups and downs
If you need to laugh
Then I'll be your clown
Look at me
If you ever feel unsure

I'm right here for you
Forever and more
Everything seems special
With you by my side
This will last forever
Till the end of time
But they say nothing lasts forever
And I know they're just wrong
They don't know our love
Is timeless like a song
I love you forever
Forever and more

4. Dreams of you

I dreamt of you again
It's all I dream of these days
It was beautiful and serene
The greatest dream that's ever been
I saw you dressed to the nines
My always forever valentine
We held hands and took flight
Like angels heading to paradise
We stared into each others soul
Saw the longing and made each other whole
There is no other place I'd rather go
Just want to be with you, with you alone
But even the best dreams
They come to an end
They always do at the best part
I can't even pretend
And just like that
The dream was snapped
My eyes opened
I didn't like that
I wanted to go back
But that way was ransacked
I sighed and hoped for fresh dreams
Something sweeter than the last one, if you please

But then I heard
You toss and turn
Right next to me
My love was snug
Fast asleep
With her own sweet dreams
Maybe about dogs and pandas
But I hope it was about me
I moved to hug her
Kiss her and hold her tight
No dream comes close to this
What I have in my life

5. Daydreaming of you at night

I've been daydreaming of you at night
Watching you bathe in filtered starlight
I want to be your lover shining bright
Oh god you make me feel so alive
With your golden glow hues
You've got me in the mood
You've got me to groove
And I've been thinking of you
And these thoughts linger all the time
There's something about you so damn sublime
And I feel lucky, so lucky
With the way you make me feel so alive
I've been daydreaming of you at night
You cleanse me of toxic thoughts
Your tears will become a desert drought
I'll be there for you day in and out
Just say the word please, you're all I've got
With your golden glow hues
You've got me in the mood
You've got me to groove
And I've been thinking of you
And these thoughts linger all the time

There's something about you so damn fine
And I feel lucky, so lucky
With the way you make me feel so alive
I've been daydreaming of you at night
I find you irresistible and I'll do what you say
I want to be better for you in every way
You always linger deep in my mind
You're so ethereal you make me feel alive
With your golden glow hues
You've got me in the mood
You've got me to groove
And I've been thinking of you
And these thoughts linger all the time
There's something about you so damn right
And I feel lucky, so lucky
With the way you make me feel so alive
I've been daydreaming of you at night

6. Her everyday battle

I see her getting spread thin
Pulled in directions she's never been
They're feeding on her soul
But she still remains whole
They keep digging at her
Trying to make her fall
But she's still standing
They've given it all
They underestimated
The size of her fight
They might win a battle or two
But winning the war is her birthright
You don't want to mess with
She's a goddess not desperate
They can do what they want
But she'll still come out on top
On the mountain of her victory
She'll claim on her own you'll see
There's nothing they can do
She's a goddess not canon fodder for you
So there's nothing you can do
To slow her down she's too good
You won't leave a scar
She's a battle born superstar

She's a pocket sized goddess
That's packed with dynamite
She's the greatest thing ever
That's happened in my life
I will fight for her if I need to
But she don't need no saving
She's not a damsel in distress
She's the boss in a cocktail dress
So you better think twice
Before crossing a line
She'll send you to hell
And she'll do it while looking divine

7. Only Her

I wake up with a frown
When she's not around
I'd like to give her a crown
She's my queen and I love the sound
Of her voice in my ears
They allay my fears
They remove my tears
I hope she's with me till the end of my years
And when she smiles I blush
And the blood goes in a rush
All to my cheeks
There's nothing quite as bleak
As the thought that she would leave
And never ever come back to me
So I'll do what I must
To keep her love and trust
And show her that my love for her
Will never ever rust
And show her that my love for her
Will never ever rust
There's no one else I want
There's no else I need
There's something about her
That's so goddamn sweet

She's got me daydreaming
About her all the time
About our future and what we'll be
It's the only thing I want, the only thing I need
And when I go to sleep
I see her in my dreams
And I'll tell you they're sweet
The sweetest they can ever be
And I don't want to imagine
A life without her around
Just the thought of it
Fills my head with disturbing sounds
And it makes me feel sick
To the bottom of my soul
She's the medicine the antidote
That makes me feel whole
I love her more than I can put in words
But I'll try my best
I'll fill a book with poems for her
And sing to her the rest
Girl you make me want to be my best
Girl you make me want to be my best

8. To my Future Wife

I know life hasn't been kind
In more ways than one
You wanted something normal
Something you thought you'd won
It's made you second guess
The happiness you deserve
It's gut punched you
And put your emotions in reserve
I know that feeling
But you've had it much worse
I know I can't be perfect
But with you I'll fight the adverse
I know how you feel about me
I've never felt so loved
I know it scares you
Because you don't have faith in god above
Because she's taken
More than she's given
And left you with fears
And left you shaken
But what I've learned in life
Is that you take what you want
Sometimes you got to ask
Sometimes you don't

Because everything worth doing
Requires a leap of faith
Whether it's spending a life together
Or dressing up for a first date
One look at you
And my heart skips a beat
One smile from you
And I'll never give in to defeat
I want to hold you close to me
And never let you go
You're my future wife for now
But in the future you'll be my heart and soul

9. Always Longing for You

Seeing you brings a smile to my face
Makes me forget my terrible day
Makes me forget that I'm a disgrace
Seeing you smile makes my heart race
I long for you when you're not around
I pass the time whistling idle sounds
My feelings spiral like a merry-go-round
I battle to keep my insecurities to ground
But I know that you won't leave
You love that I wear my heart on my sleeve
Without you all I can do is grieve
Please don't go I beg you please
Dance with me to sad slow songs
Nothing in that moment would feel wrong
I'll hold you close and twirl you around
Pick you up as high as I can off the ground
I hope that you reach for the skies
Conquer the peaks and see through lies
With you I feel so much more alive
Nothing I'd love more than for us to go on a drive
Just you and I with the moonlight by our side
Up and down hills till we're someplace inside
Warm and safe away from prying eyes
There's so much to love about you that I must summarise

All my feelings into short little songs
About how I feel all day long
I'm always longing for you when you're not around
So please stay with me forever and we'll watch the world spin round and
round

10. I love it when you spend the night

There's nothing better
Than hearing you say
I'll be there to
Spend the night and day
I rush and I panic
To clean my home
She's my queen
And my home is her throne
I'll do what I can
To make this place
Something that can
Match your grace
I know I can't wait
To kiss your face
Maybe smoke one
And travel to outer space
We'll order in
Our favourite meal
And watch something
Insane and surreal
I'll hold you close
All the time

I'm clingy you know
You blow my mind
I'll follow you around
Like a lovesick pup
I'll make some coffee
Would you like a cup?
I'll pick you up
And give you a kiss
Throw you on my bed
And kiss your lips
Both of them
And I just won't stop
We're not in a car
And there is no cop
I want you so bad
In my life
I want you to be
My, my wife
I want to be inside you
Till the end of time
Till they find our bones
Interlocked in a grind
I love it when you
Spend the night
I love it so much that
It's all I need in life
I love you more than
I can explain
I have all these words

But words can't feel the pain
Without you I feel
I'm going insane
Without you even
Sunshine feels like rain
I want to love you
Each and every day
I want to love you
In each and every way
So please please please stay
Spend each night and day
Not for long, just a lifetime I'd say
I will love you each and every day

11. The Hottest Girlfriend in the World

I love to gaze at her
Till she tells me to stop
Of course I don't
She's just too damn hot
I can't take my eyes away
It makes her blush
I tell her that I love her
That she's my crush
She maintains a decorum
That I could only wish
She holds me close
And gives me a kiss
She tells me she loves me
And then I can't contain
So I keep gazing at her
Like a lovesick puppy unchained
We could be a hinge ad
I think I'm that vain
You bring out a desire in me
That I can't explain
We look so good
We'll drive others insane

I've got the hottest girlfriend in the world
So I can't complain
She says I've gone crazy
You bet she's right
She's all I ever think about
All day and night
I'd do anything
To make her smile
To dry up her tears
I'll go the extra mile
And I have no doubt
That she's the one
She pulls on my heart strings
Gives me warmth like the sun
And I've never felt this whole
In a long long time
I want to hold you close
And whisper in your ear "You're all mine"
We could be a hinge ad
I think I'm that vain
You bring out a desire in me
That I can't explain
We look so good
We'll drive others insane
I've got the hottest girlfriend in the world
So I can't complain

12. Mine

Met you with
An open mind
Hoped for the best
From the powers divine
Didn't expect much
And it's not a lie
Not because of you
But life has been unkind
The fear
Was there
That this would
Go nowhere
It would be
Another date
Another meal
Finished in haste
We'd say our goodbyes
And fade away
From each others lives
As the night turned to day
But the universe had
Much better plans
It bought us together
As woman and man

It bound us together
By our souls
Took our incomplete halves
And made us whole
It's made me believe
In the divine
The only thing I'm sure of now
Is that you're mine!
Not for a bit
Or a while
We're in this together
For a billion more miles
We can have
Our practical doubts
We're humans
We see sunshine we see clouds
Nothing is perfect
But that's okay
There will be good memories
And there will be bad days
But nothing can stop me
From loving you like I do
How can I get bored?
When all I want out of life is YOU!
All I want in life
Is now to be
The man you deserve
But that man needs to be me
So I'll fight my demons

And slay my doubts
I will love you in sunshine
And through our darkest rain clouds
The universe has
Much better plans
It bought us together
As woman and man
It bound us together
By our souls
Took our incomplete halves
And made us whole
It's made me believe
In the divine
The only thing I'm sure of now
Is that you're mine!
Not for a bit
Or a while
We're in this together
For a billion more miles

13. Collecting stories, sunsets and sunburns with you

Hey babe
We've got a few days
Of no responsibilities
So let's pack our bags and leave
I found this place
By the beach
We can have some beer
And swim in the sea
We'll test our
Sunscreen's ability
To keep us the colour
We're meant to be
We'll share some stories
And memories
Create new ones
In the cool sea breeze
We'll watch the sunset
Over the sea
I'll keep peeking at you
Cause you're the prettiest thing I've ever seen
I'll kiss your sunburns
And I hope they heal

Girl you're so tender
But also feisty with zeal
All I want is every dream with you to turn real
We'll walk hand in hand
Between cocktails and meals
Find the next place
Where we can feel
A sense of adventure
And we can quench our thirst
We'll drink and eat
Till we're ready to burst
And get a little tipsy
Or maybe a lot
Life is more fun with you
Because you're all I've got
We'll share some stories
And memories
Create new ones
In the cool sea breeze
We'll watch the sunset
Over the sea
I'll keep peeking at you
Cause you're the prettiest thing I've ever seen
I'll kiss your sunburns
And I hope they heal
Girl you're so tender
But also feisty with zeal
All I want is every dream with you to turn real
Before we know it

We'll have to leave
Pack our bags
Put on clothes with sleeves
Go back to the city
Where we can't be free
We've got work and
A little thing called responsibilities
But it won't be long
Before we will need
A few days to ourselves
To be alone and free
Where we'll share some stories
And memories
Create new ones
In the cool sea breeze
We'll watch the sunset
Over the sea
I'll keep peeking at you
Cause you're the prettiest thing I've ever seen
I'll kiss your sunburns
And I hope they heal
Girl you're so tender
But also feisty with zeal
All I want is every dream with you to turn real

14. Obsessed

I think I was depressed
My feelings were repressed
My heartbeats were compressed
My lungs were pulled and pressed
Nothing made me impressed
I longed to be caressed
To meet you I got dressed
The lingering made me stressed
Then you walked in all bright
You shone like a light
Dispelling my darkness inside
Meeting you was a delight
We talked and gabbed all night
Kissed when no one was in sight
I wanted to hold you tight
I fought that feeling with all my might
But that feeling did stay
It stayed all night and day
I knew I needed to say
I will love you in each and every way
So I took the leap
Wrote in words too deep
I let my feelings seep
Right through me and didn't weep

I felt like I had grown
Into a man of his own
Who didn't need a loan
Who wanted to hear you moan
Each and every night
I want you by my side
You're such a delight
Even if we get into a fight
I want you to know
My feelings will always grow
I'll love you even when you're low
I'll be your warmth in the snow
My feelings are no longer repressed
I don't think I am depressed
I look at you and I'm impressed
I look at you because I'm goddamn obsessed

15. Loving you is Easy

Loving you is easy
As easy as breathing
Loving you is special
It has me believing
In a happiness filled life
With you as my wife
You're everything I could ask for
So how I can see you cry?
Or even a little sad
It makes me a little mad
To see you frown
I'll turn that frown upside down
I'll do what I can
As a mortal man
To make you smile
Even if it takes more than a while
Loving you is easy
As easy as pain
You bring sunshine in my life
Even in the rain
My love for you I can't contain
It oozes like a leaky drain
I don't know how I can explain
But loving you keeps me sane

It stops me from going insane
Your tenderness eases the pain
That life throws at me everyday
I wish I wish I could take all your pain away
And have you live in ecstasy
Without a care in a gentle breeze
You'd be free to live your wildest dreams
It's not as unlikely as it seems
I do I do I do believe
That you are here just for me
And I am bound to your soul
You complete me and I make you whole
And I'll do what I can
Without pretence
Loving you is easy
It needs no defence
I will love you forever
Even when you're down
That's when I'll be
Your counsel and your clown
I will love you forever
Even when you're low
Cause you do the same
And you help me grow
I will love you forever
Even when you're upset
You might feel grumpy
But you are still the best
I will love you forever

Even when you're annoyed
I'll do what I must
To make you overjoyed
Because loving you is easy
And I can't imagine life
Without you by my side
Without you as my future wife

16. My Love, What's got you down?

My love
What's got you down?
There's a weight on your shoulders
And it's pulling on your crown
I see you reeling, not really feeling
Like yourself
And it hurts me deep inside
Makes me wanna cry
I know sometimes
I'm the reason you're down
I can be insensitive
And behave like a clown
I promise to do better
Be a better person all around
Listen to your wants and needs
And not let you drown
In overburdened thoughts
They eat me up too
I might not be the best
Person but I'll do
What I can to be
The best person for you

You'll have your complaints
But I'll make it up to you
And not give you a reason
To stop loving me like you do
I'm only a human
But I want to be the best human for you
I'll love you with all my heart
I'll go crazy if we fall apart
I don't think I can think about
Life without you, you're all I've got
My Love, I don't know where to start
I'm sorry for how I acted out
I know you love me without a doubt
I'll love you forever, just don't leave me without…
Your love

17. Drop Dead Gorgeous

One look from you
And I go weak to my knees
One kiss from you
Has got me begging you please
Not to stop
This is all I need
Your love breaks the chains
And sets me free
You've got too much power
Over me
I love every bit of it
Don't stop please
All I think about
Is what you mean to me
All I dream about
Is being with you till eternity
You're my drop dead gorgeous
Honey, love, bae, baby
Use any word
It all means the same to me
You're mine from now
Till eternity
So let's pack our bags
And let's just leave

To a place where
It's just you and me
To a place where
It's just you and me
That's what I
Dream about
Day in
And day out
It's all I need
There's no shadow of doubt
All I need is you
You're all I think about
So let's do this
This one last dance
Let's write a chapter
On a perfect romance
A love story
That's just ours
All I want to do
Is stare at you for endless hours
Because you're my drop dead gorgeous
Honey, love, bae, baby
Use any word
It all means the same to me
You're mine from now
Till eternity
So let's pack our bags
And let's just leave
To a place where

ANKIT ARYA

It's just you and me
To a place where
It's just you and me

18. Sane Girl in a mad, mad world

They say the world is run
By mad, mad men
There's no place for a woman
Among them
They'll second guess
Talk down and look to harass
And pass a comment
On her body and her ass
They'll think she is
Nothing more than eye candy
They think they're on top
But it'll all come down you see
Because she knows what she's doing
And she knows what to say
She's got twice the battles to win
By the end of the day
And she does it all
Without breaking a sweat
She'll be remembered
And you are the people they'll forget
So throw what you want
At her if you please

There's only so much you can do
Till you'll be begging on your knees
For forgiveness
Cause she'll inherit the world
There's nothing you can do
To a sane girl in a mad, mad world
Their world is so small
The same assholes keep coming around
To fight round two
Thinking they'll win over you
They'll push the envelope
Of what they can say
They might be married
With a kid or two on the way
And they'll expect you not to complain
It's always been like this
But the world keeps changing
And revenge is a cold cold dish
Because she knows what she's doing
And she knows what to say
She's got twice the battles to win
By the end of the day
And she does it all
Without breaking a sweat
She'll be remembered
And you are the people they'll forget
So throw what you want
At her if you please
There's only so much you can do

Till you'll be begging on your knees
For forgiveness
Cause she'll inherit the world
There's nothing you can do
To a sane girl in a mad, mad world

19. The Yes behind that No

I hear your cute voice
And I think
We should have
Another drink
When I look at you
I don't want to blink
When we're married
I'm having you next to the kitchen sink
With the dirty dishes
On the side
I'll get to them I promise
I won't lie
But for now let me
Let me be inside
Let me look at you
Eye to eye
Oh god you make me
Feel so alive
Like anything is
Possible tonight
I want to feel your body
Next to mine
Let's have a quickie
Before we go out to dine

You tell me you have baggage
I'll help you carry
You might think it's a burden
But it makes me happy
Because I know you
Have this trust in me
To tell me all your fears
And fantasies
I'll do what I can
To ease your pain
But in the end we're making
Love in the rain
Oh god I can't stop thinking
About you all the time
I need you everyday
To stop me from doing unspeakable crimes
Sometimes I feel like
I'm going insane
I can't control my feelings for you
They've taken over my brain
But when I see you
Everything starts to make sense
You make it seem so easy
You love me without pretence
I look at you and wonder
How did I get this lucky?
Being loved by you
Makes me all touchy
And I'll do my best

To control my urges outside
I'll be a gentleman to the world
But your freak inside
I'll love you like
It's the only thing that matters in life
I'll love you like this
Till the day we die

20. You > Everyone Else

Some treat life
Like a buffet
People come and go
And that's okay
I've done the same
Sometimes far far worse
It feels good for a while
Until it becomes a curse
You're left empty inside
With a gaping big hole
That extends from side to side
Into your soul
Nothing seems to fill it
Until you know what you need
I need you
So darling won't you please
Hold my hand
And not let go
Stand by my side
Through pain and hope
I'm here for you
I won't let you go
I'm here forever
And forever we shall grow

I see you smile
And it unburdens me
I hear you laugh
And it sets me free
I'd choose you
Over everything
We'll make it last forever
I'm just going to get a ring
I think of you
And it makes me wanna sing
All the love songs
That I thought were cringe
But they speak to me now
In a different tongue
It's changed me from the core
All the damage's been undone
I've been born again
Into the man I've become
The man who wants to
Hold your hand and run
Away from everyone else
So we can be free
From the burdens of the world
And this society
I will love you
Till eternity
I'm bound to you
You are my destiny

21. Days I don't see you

I call them days
Of unending agony
It hurts from dawn till dusk
There is no other cure for me
I watch the clock tick tock
Every second lingers
I keep myself occupied
Twitching and cracking my fingers
The day moves so slowly
Time can be a freak
I long for the day to end
And pray tomorrow is a day you'll see me
Cause those are the days
That I'm living for
One look at you
And I learn to love forevermore
I learn more about you
It makes my feelings grow
I haven't felt this way
For a long, long time mi amor
I'll open my heart to you
And I know you'll do the same
I know I'd choose you
Over fortune and fame

But the clock keeps ticking
Now it moves so damn fast
Hours with you
Never seem to last
I push my luck
But time isn't on your side
I'll drive an hour extra
Just to get that extra time
I'll sleep a little less
To see you a little more
Anyway my dreams
Without you are a bore
We say our goodbyes
But it's only for now
We're bound together forever
Our feelings will only grow
I wake up the next morning
And the agony is back
It pinches and pulls at me
Makes the world seem so black
I patiently wait
And bide my time
Do what I can
To not lose my mind
I wait for tomorrow
Because tomorrow I'll be free
From this pain
That bothers me
It'll disappear

ONLY FOR HER

The second I see you
I love you baby
I only ever want YOU

22. Car rides to your home

One hand on the steering wheel
One hand on your thigh
I move it up your skirt
I don't want to stop tonight
You hold my hand with love and care
Tell me there are people around
We must control our urges
Even if we don't make a sound
Every traffic light
I wish to stop
So I can kiss you
Inside out
The light turns
Slowly to green
They honk behind us
And sometimes scream
The other cars whizz past us
But we're driving oh so slow
We've had a few drinks
And now we need a smoke
Something to trigger the giggles in us
Heehee ha ha I think we've had enough
I can't stop smiling when I look at you
Even when I try to act tough

We're together there's no one else
We can truly be who we are
Our vulnerabilities clearly show
They stick out like visible scars
I know it isn't easy to open yourself
We're scared we might get hurt
I just want to love you forever
And put my hand up your skirt
I've waited years
To feel like this
Every second with you
I need a kiss
Or at least a hug
And some physical touch
To reassure me that
You are all I love
We're alone in this metal box
This slow moving car
We can talk about our feelings
And who we really are
We keep opening up
On how we feel
Because this love is special
It's so damn real
That we can't stop talking
Talking about
All our fears
Dreams and doubts
We both want this

To go all the way
So we need to stay strong
This trust and loyalty will stay
I love you
In every which way
You're the best thing that happens to me
Everyday
You're the best thing
That's happened to me in this life
How could I think of anyone else
As my future wife
You're the best thing
That'll ever happen to me
I love you
Your love sets me free
We're almost at your doorstop
You tell me you don't want to go home
I know that feeling and I want you to know
We can leave right now and be somewhere alone
But life doesn't work
On our whims and fancies
I wish it did
I'd rip off your panties
And soon enough
You'll be all mine
And I'll be yours
For our lifetime
So give me a kiss
To say goodbye

I'll see you tomorrow
Under the evening sky
After we've finished
Our work for the day
I want to hold you close to me
Each and everyday

23. No More Gentleness

You've woken something in me

It's more than just love

It's quite aggressive

Its unrequited lust

I've been quite gentle

Been holding myself back

I'm not sure why

But today I end this slack

No more making love

I'm fucking you black and blue

I don't know where and how

But tonight I'm having you

Let's skip the dinner

And get a room

Down some drinks

And fuck till noon

I need you so badly

I'm losing my mind

I'm going to be forceful

Even if it's a crime

I want to be inside you

Each and every day

I want to feel your insides

In each and every way

I won't be gentle
But I'll give you a gentle kiss
It's because I love you
But there won't be any love in this
Just pure lust
And locked up desires
I've kept them chained
But they've caught on fire
You can think it's funny
The fact that I'm putting this in song
But I've made a life out of
Proving my doubters wrong
I will hold you down
Arms forcefully held to the side
I want to hear you moan
When I penetrate you inside
I won't look away
Until I turn you around
I'll have you my way
Your moans will be the sweetest sound
I'll pull on your hair
Till you scream
I'll screw you in ways
You can't even dream
I love you more than
I can put into words
But when I have you now
I don't care if you get hurt
I won't be the same

Man that you knew
I'll still be sweet and gentle
But that's not how I'll be with you
When we're all alone
I'll be a different man
A lot more feral
Something inside me I can't understand
Outside we're equals
We'll walk hand in hand
Inside you're my slave
And I'll own your ass
I'll own every bit of your
Body and flesh
I want to have you
All moist and fresh
But enough of this
Talk is cheap
You wanted me to go wild
This you've sown and this you will reap

24. I Love You

Let's walk hand in hand
And see the world together
All the pretty sunsets
And all types of weather
Carry your bikinis
And maybe some sweaters
Life's been so good
But with you it's been better
One look at you
And my heart skips a beat
One smile from you
That's what I need
To turn a day around
From bad to great
Meeting you was destined
It was in our fate
Even the stars agree
But I really don't care
All I need is you
And your ever changing hair
Your cute cute smile
Is infectious to me
I can't look away from you
So don't let me please

Let me hold you close
In happiness and in pain
Let's make happy memories
In sunshine and rain
I look at you and wonder
What good did I do
That the universe is rewarding me
A lifetime with you
I count myself lucky
The luckiest man alive
There's nothing we can't do
When we're together side to side
We'll fight the world together
And each other if there's a need
Anything to keep the love alive
Between you and me
I love you more than
I can put into words you see
I love you more than
The water in the seas
I love you more than
The sunshine and the trees
I love you more than
The winds and the breeze
I love you more than
I can see
I love you because
You make me believe
In happiness

25. A million small things and a few big things too

I've fallen for you
I'm in deep deep love with you
You know it to be true
All I think is about me and you
I'd do a million small things
And a few big things too
Anything I can I will
I will do for you
It's the big things that matter
That carry the love through
But it's the million small things
That make you say "I love you"
It could be a watch strap
That's oh so fun to play
It could be the colour white
That you like me in all day
It could be a forehead kiss
Or my hands on your thighs
I want you wrapped around me baby
All day and night
It could be my arm
Around your pretty waist

It's there to pull you close to me
So I could have a taste
I can't stop kissing you
It's become a need
I really can't stop it
I guess it's just my greed
To have you all for myself
Because you're all I ever need
I look into your eyes
And everything feels like a dream
I'll stay up a little later
Than my body can do
Don't worry I'll take a nap
Cause I want to be there for you
I'll do a million small things
And a few things too
I'll do what I can
To show you that I love you

26. Destiny

Baby I love you
And I love to see you smile
I love to see you laughing
Mind not racing at a million miles
I love to see you happy
When you're at complete ease
You give me butterflies in my tummy
Make me feel comfortable as a gentle breeze
So whenever I see you down
It hurts me deep down inside
I'll do what I can to turn that frown
Upside down, I'll be your clown
And if I am the reason
That you're feeling low
Then I will apologise
And let you know
That I love you more than
I could care to explain
I'll do what I can to make up
For your misery and your pain
Seeing you low
Makes me feel like an asshole
I don't want you to feel
That I'm not true to my soul

I'll always promise to be
Your golden retriever human being
And when you're sitting next to me
I'll hold you as close as can be
I'll be super clingy
But that's just me
I'll be your man
Because you're my destiny

27. Back to where we met

The first night we met
Is a core memory
Of happiness and everything
I wanted for you and me
We drink and dined
Looking fine
Your black dress is always
Always on my mind
We talked and talked
About everything
Your voice was music
Your words did sing
I remember looking
Into your eyes
I knew that this was
It was paradise
It's all I ever wanted
I wouldn't lie
I wanted you forever
From the very first night
That night was perfect
Wasn't it?
It was something
Made of purely bliss

And since then we can't
Get enough
Of each other
It gets really tough
On days
We don't meet
The clock ticks
To it's own beat
Life's become different
You see
You're all I have
I'm all you meet
It's just you and me
And together we're free
I love you more than I can say
You love me more than I can see
So we decided we should go
Back to where we met
So many weeks on
To relive a memory I call my best
You came dressed
All in white
Looked like an angel
From paradise
Not too different
From any other day
I can't take my eyes off you
I wouldn't have it any other way

We wined and dined
Like those many weeks ago
Now more in love
Than ever before
Talking about
Our future plans
There is some anxiety
But mostly romance
We'll deal with what
Comes our way
I need you baby forever
That's all I can say
And I'll fight for you
And I know you will too
We're destined to be together
Through and through
As the liquor
Began to flow
We felt mushy
Like we do before
Had some dessert
And some more
We kissed each other
And held each other close
What was left
Was the drive home
And some more time
For us to be alone

Car rides with you always
Feel like borrowed time
We're all alone together
But it's the end of the night
I still won't trade it for
All the riches in the world
You're all I ever wanted
So you will I always hold
Close to me
Forever if you please
I'm really obsessed with you
Darling can't you see
We take a little detour
From the sat nav route
A little break just for
Me and You
A little visit
From the garden of green
Something that makes our mind
Giggle but stay clean
We stopped for a moment
To have a moment for ourselves
A moment we're alone
With no one else
But the moment didn't last long
The fuzz got in the way
The hustled bustled us
For our hard earned pay
It could have been much worse

But the universe was kind
They understood that we're in love
And not just killing time
They let us go
We were on our way
Not looking back
Not looking to stay
The fear passed
Only giggles prevailed
I love you my baby girl
That's all I can say
This is another
Core memory for us
The day we relived our first date
But it was better than the first
As we say our goodbyes
We held each other tight
I'll love you forever
Baby please sleep well, goodnight

28. Full Circle

Life come full circle
It moves in loops
We went back where we first met
Where I first saw you
Things had changed
We had grown
We learned so much about each other
But still so much we need to know
I get scared sometimes
Because I know this is so real
But then I meet you for dinner
And that becomes my new favourite meal
The anxieties leave my body
My mind becomes clear
Looking at you look at me
You're everything I hold dear
You lay out your fears
And you do it with ease
You only do this
Because I know you love me
I love you so much
It hurts at times
Time away from you is painful
Because I know you're mine

I look at you and I see
My future and my present
I want to hold you forever
And not make you resent
Time with me today
Or any tomorrow
I've grown to love you
In your happiness and sorrow
I want to take care of you
And have you take care of me
I'm not perfect not by a long shot
But I know I want to be
As perfect as I can
So I can be
Someone worthy of your love
Be the man of your dreams
In many ways I know
The honeymoon phase is over
What I'm left with now is feelings for you
That make me want to hold you closer
I see you for the beautiful
Person that you are
Someone I can't stop loving
Someone who heals my scars
This is more real
Than I thought it could be
You make me feel special
And it puts my heart at ease
You're the only person

That I want with me
For the rest of our lives
You're the only one I need
Life comes full circle
It moves in loops
I thought I just loved you
But I feel more than that for you

29. It's getting real

My emotions had gone numb
They were buried deep within
I didn't think I had them anymore
I was just livin'
One day at a time
No future on my mind
Just living life with horse blinds
Only seeing what's ahead and not what's beside
It got so tiresome
I felt so lonely
I'd forgotten about love
The idea of a one and only
They all seemed like distant ideas
Very vague thoughts
The depression was killing me
Inside and out
I had to build myself back up
One brick at a time
It was slow and painful
But it felt so right
I'm still a work in progress
But I guess I'll never be done
I'll always try and be better
For the girl I love

She came out of nowhere
Into my life
I never thought this girl
Would be my future wife
Now I can't imagine
A life where she's not there
She's melted my heart
And given me someone to care
About
Day in and day out
There is no shadow of doubt
She's the one that my life's all about
And it makes me want to shout
Out in happiness
"I've found her"
I've found my princess
But this is not the end
Of this story
It's just the start
Of the girl who adores me
I just want to see her happy
And not be stressed
Because I've been there
I've been depressed
You stop being yourself
You don't do what you like
You become your own enemy
Out of spite
I can't have her go through this

Not even a bit
I love her too much
I'll do what I can to stop all of it
All her suffering is now mine
It's my personal enemy
She can handle it alone
But I will always be
By her side
To help her through
We're going through this life together love
Just me and YOU

30. You make me all mushy

Every morning I wake up
With a smile
I think about you
For a while
It's a good way to start
Each and everyday
You'd wake up next to me
If I could have my way
And I will I'm sure
Just watch and wait
Then I'll be mushy with you
From morning till it's late
You're about to get smothered
Day in and out
You'll love it but you'll ask me
If I could stop?
Of course I can't
But I say I will
I'll try my best
I'll be lying still
Because I can't stop
All this mushiness
You're too adorable
So I can't rest

I need you more than
I could say
But my actions will show you
How I feel about you babe
It's a mixture of love
And a whole lot of lust
I'll smother you with kisses
And a few love bites are a must
You make me all mushy
All gooey inside
I feel like these feelings
Will stay awhile
Probably a lifetime
If not more
God damn I love you
You are the only one I adore
So just get used to this
That's all I can say
I'm not going to act differently
That's not my way
I wear my feelings
On my face
And what it says
Is that I want you each and everyday
You're my sunshine
During my raincloud moods
You're the only one I know
Who can make me feel like I do
And I do feel happy

Deep within my soul
You've helped me fill
This gaping hole
I had in me
For the longest time
There's something you
That's so damn fine
You make me all mushy
All gooey inside
I feel like these feelings
Will stay awhile
Probably a lifetime
If not more
God damn I love you
You are the only one I adore

31. I Love Her

It's just a simple feeling
But it's oh so deep
It's got me down kneeling
For the girl I want to keep
Beside me for a lifetime
Not a day less than that
She's the only one that can keep me
From losing myself to the black
And empty void inside my mind
It pulls me down all the time
She picks me up with her smile
Gives me a reason to feel alive
I feel so loved
And tended to
The dark side of my mind
Says she'll abandon you too
But one look at her
And I feel so assured
I fight the darkness in me
Because being with her is the cure
And it's working well
And I'm staying sane
Looking well
And acting vain

We look so good together
This girl and I
I love her to death
Because she makes me feel alive
We're the talk of the town
Of course jealousy is abound
We're oh so perfect
So perfectly sound
I pray to the gods
And the energies
To keep us safe
From our enemies
And well wishers
Who don't wish so well
I see them all around
I wish they go to hell
I'm with her till the end
I love her and I can't pretend
Any other feelings except the ones I have
She's the one I want because she's all that
And so much more
I can't get enough
Of this feeling
We call love

32. Cutest, Prettiest, Hottest, Sexiest

She's got the cutest smile
It drives me crazy all this while
She's got me wondering deeply
If she's put a trance on me
She's got the prettiest face
Full of life and it's exuding grace
She's got me thinking all the time
About how I'm lucky that she's all mine
She's got the hottest body on her
I want to strip her naked and cover her in fur
She's got me wanting to be wrapped up with her
If love is a medicine then she's the cure
She's the sexiest person alive
She's my girlfriend and future wife
She's got me dancing to her tunes
Look at my Spotify you'd think I'm a swiftie like you
Writing for and to you
Is my therapy
There's no other medicine
That I need
I look at you
And I feel oh so free

Happiness feels possible
Between you and me
I'll say this now
And whenever you need
I love you babe
You're better than my dreams
You're right here
Right in front of me
Whenever I wake up
I want you next to me asleep
She's got the cutest smile
It drives me crazy all this while
She's got me wondering deeply
If she's put a trance on me
She's got the prettiest face
Full of life and it's exuding grace
She's got me thinking all the time
About how I'm lucky that she's all mine
She's got the hottest body on her
I want to strip her naked and cover her in fur
She's got me wanting to be wrapped up with her
If love is a medicine then she's the cure
She's the sexiest person alive
She's my girlfriend and future wife
She's got me dancing to her tunes
Look at my Spotify you'd think I'm a swiftie like you

33. Baby And Broccoli Chapter 1

They met on a
Fateful night
After many days of speaking
The occasion seemed right
There were no expectations
But broccoli had some hopes
A hope that this could be
A relationship that could grow
But he had had
No such luck
Not for years
Dating can suck
Baby ran a little late
Rush hour made Broccoli wait
He could do nothing
So he had a drink and ate
Broccoli dressed up at work
The best he could do
He had a lot of nerves
But something that beer would soothe
It calmed him down
And made him assured

He was now ready
To not be a bore
Baby was almost there
And Broccoli hoped
That this would be an evening
That the kids would describe as dope!
Baby got off
At the wrong street
Wasn't very far
But had to make it on her own feet
Those heels didn't help
And she did her best
To move along quickly
But soon she'd need rest
Broccoli waited outside
Trying to look his best
This could be it
He said under his breath
He saw her at a distance
And went to her
He saw she was everything
He had hoped for
Baby was decked up
To the nines
Looking so exquisite
Wanting to sip on wine
He held her and
Passed a smile
Let's get some drinks

And sit a while
They sat across the table
And spoke with ease
Let's have another drink she said
If you please
The conversation flowed
And so did the drinks
This was going too well
He started to think
They waited in line
To use the loo
He looked deep in her eyes and said
I want to kiss you
She smiled at him
And looked in the mood
Don't worry she said
You'll get to
Broccoli used
The facilities
Stepped out and saw her
Waiting for he
She walked to him
And he to her
They met in the darkness
And he kissed her
This was the start
Of something sweet
So they did what they could
They just wanted to meet

Each other
And never stop
It's still the same
It's who they are
This was chapter 1
Of Baby and Broccoli
About the most important night
The night they finally did meet

34. God I just need to see you

You're so close

Yet so far

It's not the distance

It's the hours

Not seeing you

Exposes my scars

Makes me behave in ways

Not fit for who we are

I think I'm obsessed

That's for sure

Part of it is a good thing

The other part is a definite no

I'm sorry if I act

Crazy at times

I'm crazy in love with you

But I still need to behave right

I feel kind of rotten

But I don't want you to be sad

I'll learn to be better

And not make you mad

Not put you in a position

Where you have to choose

Between doing what's needed

And what you want but is of no use

All I know for sure
Is that I love you
But I can't behave like this
Definitely not with you
God I just need to see you
But the wait will hardly be a day
But it'll feel like eternity
Cause I feel myself slipping away
But I'll be fine
I know that for sure
I have you to help me
Pick myself up off the floor

35. I'm fighting with myself

Barely being able
To keep it together
I'm fighting with myself
To make myself better
I don't want you to see
This struggle in me
It might scare you
Or you might think I'm diseased
I wish this wasn't
A part of me
But I have to learn to live with it
Or I'll never truly be free
All in all
I'm doing mostly fine
Doing my best
Not committing any crimes
I wish I was with you
You make me feel safe
You keep me in the light
Where I can't see my dark face
I'll tell you the truth
I'm very very scared
Because if I lose you
I don't think I would care

About the things
I usually do
A part of me will die
It'll be gone too soon
I'll keep living
For the world to see
But I'll be dead inside
As dead as can be
I'm just a damaged soul
But you might be one too you know
I don't want to be alone
I need you my love, I need you to know
I'm scared of what
Could become of me
I'm strong and I'll fight this
But sometimes I'm weak
I'm just a human
I wish I was so much more
But I've been given something
I cherish and adore
I have your love
And it's more than I need
But please please please
All of it I want to keep

36. Baggage

My body is full of vigour
But my mind is drained
The whole world around me is fine
But everything seems strained
Everything seems like it's on fire
And it's burning me up inside
It's all in my head that's true
But if it feels so real then how is it a lie?
I hate that you have to see this
But it can't stay buried forever
Oh god I sound so dramatic
It's not how I act ever
Well maybe sometimes
But not to this degree
I think that's something
We all can agree
I have my baggage
It's because I'm insecure
I know I have your love
But it can't be the cure
I fear I'll be abandoned
And left all alone
That's why I see the world like I do
But I can't live like this anymore

I can't go in circles
Making the same mistakes
I can't lose you or myself
I'll do what it takes
To be the best version of me
And maybe even better than that
If there's one thing you've taught me
It's that we'll always have each others back
But our battles are our own
And that's always true
It's like I always say
Life is the world vs yourself vs you
I know you have your baggage
And I'm there to lighten your load
I don't want you to feel like
You're all alone
I know that feeling
And it eats me up inside
I'm going to face my demons
And not run and hide
I love you too much
To ever lie
I hope you feel the same way
Like how I do deep inside

37. You're So Amazing

I feel the darkness subside

In it I don't want to reside

The pain is still there

But it's easier to hide

I'd give it sometime

Maybe a night

But I'm sure I'll be

Back to who I was in your mind

You're so amazing

And I think you should know

There's no one else in the world

With whom I want to grow

I'll give you more reasons to stay

Than to leave

I'll stand by you

When you need relief

I'll be your protector

But never your saviour

You're too good for me anyway

So I'll just watch my behaviour

You're so amazing

And I think you should know

There's no one else in the world

With whom I want to grow

I want to wrap you
In my arms
Hold you close
Protect you from harm
Cause you do
The very same
You hold me like
I'm yours to tame
I love it to bits
I kid you not
You scare me a little
But that's because I love you a lot
You're so amazing
And I think you should know
There's no one else in the world
With whom I want to grow

38. This Girl I Love

This girl I love

Is all that she can be

But there is so much more

I can see

She's got the cutest smile

And a cuter voice

How can I love someone else

There is no other choice

She loves to taunt

And she does it so well

She slips it in conversation

Takes you from heaven to hell

She loves to show affection

When we're all alone

You can see it in her eyes

She makes you feel like you're sitting on a throne

I wish that she

Would never get sad

Never feel anything

That'd make her mad

But the good always comes

With the bad

Then all I wish is to be there

And do what I can

To make her feel like
She's on top of the world
Hold her close
And spin her in a twirl
Show her that
I'm all hers
She belongs to me
And I'm owned by her
When she's down
I feel the weight of the world
On my shoulders
I just want to hurl
This feeling away
So I can do what I can
To make her feel like
There's nothing that her man
Won't do to put a smile
On her face
I would do anything
To put her in her place
Which is at
The top of it all
She's my everything
Everything else doesn't matter at all
All my dreams
Are about being with her
The only thing better
Is waking up next to her
And holding her close

Right up to me
Kissing her nonstop
Before she can get up to pee
She asks me to stop
But it's not something I can do
This girl I love
Is someone I almost never knew
It's funny how life
Does it's thing
Brings people together
Makes them buy a ring
Shows them life
Can feel like a dream
The girl I love
Is my forever queen

39. You mean the world to me

Seeing you down

Brings me down to my lowest point

Makes me want to rush to you

And smoke a joint

A little something to

Lighten the mood

Turn your frown upside down

Is something I'd like to do

We could go on a drive

Get some ice cream

Mint chocolate chip for you

And something for me too

That you could take a bite off

If you please

Everything I do is about you

Can't you see

You mean the world to me

And I haven't felt like this before

You mean the world to me

And sometimes you mean more

I dream about you all the time

Sometimes in the day

Sometimes in the night
All of them are happy and bright
Like your hair everyday
It reminds me of the sun on a rainy day
It brings me fire it brings me warmth
It brings me everything that I want
Sometimes I'm not sure
Of what I can do
To make you feel better
But I'll still keep trying for you
Sometimes it'll be a song
Sometimes it'll be a treat
Sometimes I'll just show up on your doorstep
And say we're going to eat
So put something on
We're leaving now
We're going on an adventure
So play your favourite songs
You mean the world to me
And I haven't felt like this before
You mean the world to me
And sometimes you mean more
You're the sunshine in my raincloud
My island in the sea
My oasis in the desert
That's what you mean to me
The days I see you are good
All the others are meh
When you say we can't meet

All I can say is okay
But inside I feel so distraught
I'm all on fire
I don't like those days
But it fuels my desire
To be the best I can
On the days we meet
All I think about is
What you mean to me
You mean the world to me
And I haven't felt like this before
You mean the world to me
And sometimes you mean more

40. Considerate

I need to be more considerate
About how you feel
Sometimes I get lost in the moment
And forget what's real
You've been supportive
And everything I could ask
The least I can do
Is be up to the task
Of taking care of you
And asking how you are
Ask you about your day
And your open scars
You're special to me
And I cannot let go
Of doing something wrong
And it's something I know
Hurting you is the
Last thing on my mind
You ask nothing of me
And give me all your time
Sometimes I know
I will make these mistakes
But the thing I want to do right
Is rectify and I'll do what it takes

To let you know that I
Love you with all my heart
I can't see you hurt and angry
It tears me apart
You're what life is worth living for
I'll do what I can
When I go wrong I'll apologise
Because I'm no superman
I don't know if you'll forgive this
But I hope that you do
All that I can say for sure
Is that I love you

41. Love you the hardest

I'll love you the hardest
Especially when you're low
This is something about me
That you should know
Love to me is sacred
And you are as holy as can be
I don't want you to sleep angry
So please talk to me
I'm all ears and I'll do
What's needed and more
I won't give you up
And I'll fight for you I'm sure
Loving you is the most
Important thing to me
Understanding your pain and anger
Is needed for me to see
Where I went wrong
And what I can do
To make you feel like
You're the most important person in the room
Because that's how I feel
About you all the time
I want you to be happy
And I'll fix the wrong that I've

Done and I'll do it
Every single day
Because you matter to me
More than I can say
I don't want to go to sleep
Knowing you feel this way
I don't want you to feel
This way at the end of the day
Talk to me please
And open up on how you feel
Please do this for me
This love to me is real
I'll love you at your lowest
Even if you don't want it from me
I'll do what I can to make you feel better
Because nothing else matters to me
I love you more than
I could ever say
Because words are great
But they get in the way
Of how I truly feel
And I know it in my heart
That you're the girl for me
The girl who I love in light and dark

42. These feelings I feel

These feelings I feel for you
And deeper than the ocean floor
I wish I could love you
Even much more
I can't grow tired of you
You're everything I adore
Love to me is not a honeymoon phase
Because I want you forevermore
You're the light at the end of the tunnel
For my life has been darkness
You're the warmth that I bask in
The soul that stopped me from being heartless
It pains me to see you in any pain
It pains me even more when I can't explain
How I feel to have let you down
Even if it's for a moment, it makes me want to drown
I don't wish to write
Tomes of love for you everyday
But they leak out of me
Like the words I want to say
You're the starlight that guides me
Through the night
You're the fire that keeps me warm
That keeps my soul alight

You give me purpose
More than I did
You give me the love
That even god can't forbid
Your love teaches me
To be the very best
Your laughter teaches me
To take joy in jest
These feelings I feel for you
Are a part of my soul
They complete me
They make me whole
I only wish
That you could know
This love I have for you
Will always grow

43. Baby and Broccoli Chapter 2

Now it has been
Many moons
Since they first met
And since then they knew
That this is worth
The time and space
Not everyday is easy
But it's worth the wait
Baby comes with
Baggage of her own
Sometimes it's towering
Like a heavy stone
Broccoli has issues
All in his mind
It's a fragile place
That wants to commit crimes
He can be clingy
But that's all he knows
She can be hurtful
But somehow the love grows
There are days
That are not so great

In their minds
Love can turn to hate
He'll do what he can
To fight for his love
Even if she pushes him away
With a shove
She's fighting too many
Battles to count
Some are at work
Some she can surmount
She needs some space
From time to time
He'll give her all that
But love has to be reciprocated in his mind
She doesn't mean it
But sometimes it hurts
He puts all he has for her
But sometimes she's just too curt
Maybe he should
Tone it down
But how do you not put the love out
That you have just found
He needs to learn
His partners ways
How she lives her life
And how her mind operates
He doesn't like how
She is at the start of her day
He's already up

And on his way
There is love
But this will take
Efforts and patience
But it'll be worth the cake
He is not the best
To put in words he speaks
About everything in his mind
And how he feels
They can have
A terrible effect
He loves her madly
But his words he must select
She will wear
Her emotions on her face
She can look at you with love
She can look at you with hate
She knows what she wants
And that's what she'll take
Does she want his heart and soul?
For that we must wait
I guess these are
Two different souls
They love each other
And together they can be whole
But for this to work
They need to grow
Not just by themselves
But together they must show

What they're willing to do
For each other each day
Sometimes it's more
Than the other can take
Broccoli loves baby
More than he can say
He's willing to hurt himself
To make her happy each day
Baby loves broccoli
Clear as the day
She's willing to lose her sleep and sanity
Just so that he can have his way
But what is their future
We must ask
There is something here
It's more than a spark

44. I'm here only

Seeing you feeling not quite like yourself
Makes me miss you even more
If there was only something I could do
To make you feel like this feeling would go
And sooner than later you'll feel like yourself
You'll feel like who you really are
The one that goes to work and conquers
Everyone in her way with permanent scars
And I'll be here only when you call
Waiting in my car
Together we'll go on another adventure
Seeking ourselves and who we are
In this mad mad world
That's always in a rush
The only thing I know is that I love you
And you're still my crush
We got so much to do
And so little time
It's really not much
Just a whole lifetime
Sometimes stars don't align
But do they really matter in our mind
I see you and you see me
We'll do what's needed so we can be free

From expectations of other souls
Some are well wishers some assholes
But we both know what's to be done
We're in this together because we know we're one
And I'll be here only when you call
Waiting in my car
Together we'll go on another adventure
Seeking ourselves and who we are
In this mad mad world
That's always in a rush
The only thing I know is that I love you
And you're still my crush
We got so much to do
And so little time
It's really not much
Just a whole lifetime
Take some rest
And find some peace
The lack of it will bring you
Down to your knees
I can't see you in any pain
It hurts me too much I can't explain
Maybe it's just that time of the month
But baby please get better I love you too much
And I'll be here only when you call
Waiting in my car
Together we'll go on another adventure
Seeking ourselves and who we are
In this mad mad world

That's always in a rush
The only thing I know is that I love you
And you're still my crush
We got so much to do
And so little time
It's really not much
Just a whole lifetime

45. The Stars aren't always right

I do believe in god

I know you don't

You think of her as a fraud

I think of her as a light that won't

Go out off this world anytime soon

Will guide you where you need to go

Especially when you're down

Especially when you're low

But I'm not a blind believer

I only believe cause I've seen her

Pull me out from the darkness I was in

Made me the man who made you think

Maybe I can give marriage another chance

This boy makes me want to hold him and dance

And we'll dance through life hand in hand

We'll discover what is true romance

And I know you're feeling low

Because the stars they say that we won't last

But what do they know?

About our future or our past

They were right once before

But what do they really know?

We grow as people and we let go
Of our anger and the things that don't help us grow
They can read our charts
And pick us apart
But they can never know
Who we truly are
The people we meet
And the life we live
Shapes us in ways
That makes us forgive
Others and ourselves in part
We become who we truly are
Not something the stars can see
They can be right but they really don't know me
So I've been praying to god
It's not something I do a lot
But I've been feeling the need
The need for my mind to be freed
Off the shackles that have been placed
On me and you by ones who say
They know everything about this life
And universe and have the answers we need to find
I don't believe them
Nor do I think they lie
They just don't know us
Not even if they tried
I believe in god and she'll guide me
To find the truth about the one I seek
I know it's you I feel it in my soul

Without you my life will have a big black hole
What I've learned in this life
The stars aren't always right
They can guide us through the night
But it's for us to live and fight
For what we want in this world
I want you and nothing more
I will do what I can
To show whomsoever matters that I'm your man
There's nothing that can keep us apart
If you want this like me then I'll do my part
In proving the stars wrong, no matter what it takes
I love you girl, with you a life I want to make

46. Making things right

For me to make things right
I know it'll take time
Words aren't enough
When my actions are my crimes
I can't thank you enough
For giving me another chance
I'll make it worth your while
This won't be our last dance
I behaved like a fool
Because my heart was in pain
You weren't wrong
But I felt like I was going insane
I've hurt you more than I
Ever imagined I could do
It's not something I wanted to
Because I truly love you
You can call these words lies
And I won't blame you if you do
But one thing you can't deny
Is how I feel about you
I'm a loner in this world
Not too many people I speak to
I don't really open up
Unless I really need to

But I stick to the surface
Of who I really am
I'm scared to let the world know
That my confidence is a scam
I'm still that scared kid
Who mumbles while he speaks
All this surface level shine
Is to hide that I am weak
But I can't hide myself from you
You need to know who I am
I love more than I can
Ever understand
There's something about you
That I find oh so sweet
You've let me in your heart
You let me sweep you off your feet
And I hurt you in ways
That makes me want to cry
How could I be so cruel?
To the person I want for the rest of my life
Everyday I long to see you
But I will have to wait
I need to learn to be patient
Otherwise your love for me will turn to hate
I know you'll need time
To forgive me for what I've done
I deserve every bit of it
But I promise I won't run
I love you with all my heart

And it's the whole damn truth
There's no other girl for me
There's only just YOU
I wish I could
Turn back the days
Undo all my
Ghastly mistakes
But time only moves forward
I've learned that in this life
So I'll keep moving ahead
Till I make you my wife
You'll see the new me
I promise you this
These won't be just words
My actions will be bliss
I will behave how I should have
All this very time
I was just too excited
To have found the love of my life
I will calm your anxieties
Like you have mine
You're the girl for me
Only person worth my time
I hope you forgive me one day
Truly in your heart
I know it'll take a while
But I'll be waiting patiently for it in the dark

47. Fuck the Universe

We've been waiting
To see each other again
But the universe is playing
A game with us of pain
I long to see you
Hold you close to me
I need to kiss you
Have you next to me
Every waking moment
Every moment we're asleep
I want you by my side
I am yours to keep
But life isn't always
Going to be like this
So the universe does
Things to make us flip
And curse the situation
I do it all the time
I need to see you
Or I feel like I'll lose my mind
But enough of these dramatics
We'll be holding each other soon
We'll be snuggled in a blanket
In my comfy room

We'll have all this time together
Now and forever
I'll hold you close to me
Never let you be
Lost in thought about us
If this is what he wants
I want you forever
And maybe more if that counts
But every day waiting
Hurts me in my soul
I know you want me there with you
Caressing you whole
I wish I had a teleportation
Machine I could use
I would appear next to you
And take you with me on a cruise
We'd teleport and travel
The world all around
I'd kiss you everywhere
And we'd disappear without a sound
But enough of these dreams
I have a better one
You and I together forever
Walking in the sun
On a sandy beach
And on a city road
In whatever place we are
I want you to know
I love you now

And forever in time
You're the only one for me
You're the better half of my life

48. The girl I want to marry

She's handsy and frisky
But she's got a tender heart
She loves it when I
Spread her legs apart
Trying to have a quickie
With her everyday
Especially before
We have to be on our way
To meet other people
As life would have us do
What I really want is
To spend every night with you
Cuddled in together
In a blanket that's too big
But you'll still pull it
Off me very quick
You'll corner me on the bed
Have me dangling on the side
But you know what love
I love every bit of it, I can't lie
Thinking about the future
With you has me all smiles
This is all I want in life
To have you by my side
Together we'll have
Many adventures and tales to tell
This girl I want to marry
Is all I want or else life would be hell

49. Morning musings of love

Love comes in many ways
But it always wants you to stay
It teaches you to be better
Than you were yesterday
It teaches you patience
It tests your understanding
It teaches you the value
Of not being that demanding
It's the connection of two souls
That together want to be whole
And bring the best out of each other
And love each other without control
I see you in my dreams
It's almost always serene
I want you forever
I want you next to me
I want to hold your hand
And grab you by your waist
I want to love you forever
I know it's not in haste
I've done so much wrong
I'll put it all in song
I need you more than ever
To love me and tell me I belong

Deep in your heart
Entangled in your soul
I wish I was perfect
Perfectly in control
But we're just humans
And humans do err
But don't ever think
That I don't care
You're all I think about
When my mind is clear of doubt
You're so special to me
That you I can't live without
I love you because you found
A way into my heart
I thought it was made of stone
But the stone you took apart
Now you see me
The real human inside
All I do is feel for you
And these feelings don't lie
I want you to be happy
And I'll do what I can
To always make you laugh
To always be your man
Nothing makes me happier
Than watching you smile
And holding me close to you
For more than a while
I want you to miss me

When I'm not around
Cause when I'm not with you
I crave for the sound
Of your voice and your giggles
My soul they tickle
I wish my ego
Wasn't this brittle
I don't want to lose you
And I know I won't
Because I won't give up on our love
I'm not a quitter and I don't
See a life without you
That'll make me happy
You are the reason
My life isn't crappy
I love waiting for you
In my car
I love waiting even more
At our favourite bar
I love seeing you waking up next to me
I blush when you do
I won't stop looking at you like I do
How could I ever stopping loving you?
I'll do what I can
To not lose you
Because losing is the dumbest
Thing I could do
You fight for me I know
You'll fight the world if need be

I'll do the same you do know
Because you're the one who's set me free
You've helped me break these chains
All they did was contain
The real me from the world
I'm free now and free to explain
The love I feel for you
Is deeper than the depths
Of the ocean
And higher than Mount Everest
And now I end my
Morning musings of love
My coffee is finished
There's vigour in my blood
I'll start my day of work
But I'll keep you in my heart
You are the reason
I want to create art
You are my muse
My reason for creation
I love you so much
That I don't see this as recreation
My words for you
Are exactly how I feel
Sometimes I'm terrible at speaking
But my writings always clear
They're a window to my soul
And inside it is you
Holding me together

ONLY FOR HER

With your love and some glue

50. One more day of waiting

The universe is testing us
More than it should
Every step closer we take
Another step the universe puts
But it's all a feeling in the moment
I know it'll fade away
The second we see each other
It wouldn't matter anyway
Spending the night with you
Is the only thing I crave
But I crave it so much
I want it everyday
I know you do too
But I guess we have to wait
It'll happen trust me
I don't care what the stars have to say
You're so perfect
I still can't believe
That I'm with the person
Of my dreams
Everyday I pinch myself
To see if I'm still asleep
But even when I am
You're the only person about who I dream

I just want to pamper you
And have you do the same
I'd choose you over
All the fortune and fame
But I want that too
Just for us
So we can do what we dream off
But still work off our butts
We look so good together
A match made by the gods
We complete each other
Erase each others faults
I miss your smile
And your little tiny quirks
You're so goddamn adorable
I look at you and smirk
I thank the gods and the universe
For making me the luckiest man
I have your love and attention
What more can I ask?
I can't wait to see you again
And have the time of our lives
Then go back home
Where I have a small surprise
Nothing too big
Just your favourite treat
Just some mint chocolate chip ice cream
Waiting for you to eat
I might ask for a bite

But you can have it all
God I love you so much
You're the one worth fighting for
We got one more day of waiting
To see each other at last
I'm counting down the hours
While reminiscing the past

51. Half princess half menace

She's got a wicked smile
And a cute laugh
You put it together
And she's always a blast
She's got my attention
She's the only one I want
She's the one with who
I've got the special bond
She makes me feel special
And I don't know how
She's the one for me
The one I want now
And tomorrow
And the day after that
I want her forever
Forever till the world turns to black
She's the girl of my dreams
But in real life
I want to marry her
I don't need to think twice
What is it about her?
That's just so sweet
Every moment with her
Feels like a treat

She makes me feel special
And I don't know how
She's the one for me
The one I want now
And tomorrow
And the day after that
I want her forever
Forever till the world turns to black

52. I always have the best time when I'm with you

The best days in my life
Are the ones when you are by my side
The best days of my life
Will be when you are my wife
I'm addicted to your love
I'm enchanted by your soul
I know I want you
Because you make me lose control
You bring out the
Best part of me
The one who knows how to love
And how to be
A kind loving man
That's not really who I am
But maybe it is
And now he has a plan
For you and I to be
In love till we breathe
To live together on our own
So we can be free
I always have the best time
When I'm with you

It's a feeling I know
I only get from you
You make me feel weak
In my knees
Your kisses caress me
Like a cool summer breeze
I want you to know my
Love for you is deep
There's something about you
That makes me want to scream
And tell the world I love
This girl she's my dream
So everyone else back away
She is mine to keep
I will love her till the end
The end of days
I will cherish her love
Till I don't know what to say
I will treat her like the princess
I know she is for me
She's the girl who taught me
To always believe
In myself and us
And that's what I'll do
I'll be her man with a plan
And tell her I'm with you
Through thick and thin
And right and wrong
I'm with you

I'll write a song
About how we will overcome
The obstacles from which we can't run
And I will love you because you're the one
And I am the moon to your sun

53. I'm obsessed with how hot we are

I think about you
All the time
When I got nothing running
In my mind
You're deep in there
Looking fine
With an overdose
Of the divine
I know you're scared
Of doing this one more time
You're brave and definitely
Not out of your mind
I haven't had another person
Who I could call mine
I haven't had one
In a long long time
Adventures with you
Are now my life
I just want you forever
As my wife
The stars don't agree
With us I believe

But something about it
I just don't agree
Feels like the universe
Is stacked against you and me
They can try and do
Do as they please
I'm obsessed with how
Hot we are
Especially when we
Drive around in my car
Showing the world
How good we look
They'll write about us
In romance books
I'll hold your hand
And not let go
Give it a gentle squeeze
And I kiss it so you know
You belong to me
I own your soul
The flesh is mine too
But I'll give you more
I see you for
Who you are
A beautiful girl
With a beautiful heart
You have your fears
And I'll do my best
To help you overcome some

And assuage the rest
I want you in every way
And I mean that for sure
Life had brought me down
You were the cure
The least I can do
Is make you feel the same way
About how you I feel about you
All night and day
I wish you could see you
Through my eyes
You'll see all this love
That I have for you in my mind
And all these thoughts about you
That are dancing around
In my brain
Going round and round
I'm obsessed with how
Hot we are
I'm obsessed with you
Obsessed by your love
I'm obsessed with how
Hot we are
All I want is you and me
Driving around in my car

54. Process

Love is not easy
It takes effort and heart
It's easy to be together
Difficult to stay apart
Sometimes it comes at us
Way too fast
We don't have to process
What we really want
These feelings scare me
Day in and day out
I've learned to live with them
Because in the end you're all I want
I can fight a million battles
For you if that's what you want
Or I'll surrender in a moment
If I'm not in your heart
But such decisions
Aren't taken for the fuck of it all
You really need to think about
Where you want life to take you after all
We have our baggage
And we can carry it together
Help each other unpack it
And feel a lot better

But some of it is
A personal battle
You need to handle it alone
Something we all must tackle
I know you have days
Where your mind is in doubt
Whether you want any of this
Or just want to disappear from it all
So you take the time
To process what you want
I still love you
When you're not around
But my love will stay
Only till it lasts
It can be forever
But you can also be the past
I love you
With all my heart
Not being with you
Tears me apart
But I can't rush you
In processing your thoughts
I know you love me
But love is more than what's in our hearts
I'll wait for you patiently
And hope you feel how I do
I'm ready to take on the world
But only just for YOU
Love for me has no limits

But only if it's given back
You know what my love
You've done just that
You've loved me
With all your heart
But I know it's scary
What if this all falls apart?
Neither of us were ready
To feel this way
At least not this fast
And I don't know what to say
To reassure you
And make you feel safe
All I can tell you
Is I dream of your face
When I go to sleep
Late into the night
You're always in my thoughts
You're always a delight
You're the one who's made me
Feel like I'm alive
Before this I felt dead
Or just living out of spite
I'm not the easiest
Person to love
But you've loved me
Like an angel from above
So take your time
I'll be waiting for you for as long as I can

Process what's in your mind
I always want to be your man
I want to love you forever
And forever if I can
I will love you forever
If you choose me as your man

55. Away from you

Being away from you
Makes me want you more
I'm not talking about your body
I'm talking about your soul
God I can't stop loving you
I want to more and more
What is this astrology shit?
I just want you as my amore
You might feel differently
But I still feel the same
You're the one I want
You're my eternal flame
I don't care how I sound
I'm saying it like it is
I might be drunk and out of bounds
But this is what it is
I love you baby
You're all I ever need
I don't care what it takes
I'll stay with you if you please
I don't want to think about
Life without you
You're the reason I am
So happy and it's true

I can't stop thinking about
And what you mean to me
I don't care how I sound
I want you to be
With me forever
And I'll do what it takes
You're the only for me
And the one who makes
Me a better man
And it's all I'll ever need
Except I need you
To be the one that keeps
Me all together
In one piece
I love you more than I can
Describe in a scene
And now I end this
Very drunk post
I love you I do
I love you the most

56. I'll wait for you

I know the world

Is weighing down on you

You're not yourself right now

And it feels like there's nothing you can do

It's not fair that all this pressure

Comes raining down on you

But I know you'll get through this

Because you always do

You're not a quitter

Not even one bit

You always come out on top

Dusting yourself off saying "is that it?"

I wish life didn't throw

These curveballs at us

But I'm willing to fight

If my love you trust

We're quite different

You and I

But that's not a bad thing

We're like the water and sky

We compliment each other

And fix our broken parts

We can sand out our roughness

But it won't happen if we're apart

We don't need to rush
Into anything
We can take our time
And see what we think
About each other
And see how strong is the love
We might get a blessing
From the powers above
I can't see the future
No one can
But I see the present
Where I want to be your man
I wish I could help you
Through all of this
But I can still love you
No matter the risk
Please speak to me
Your silence hurts too much
I wish you were next to me
Because I want to touch
You on your cheek
And pull you in for a kiss
Tell you how I feel
And how you make my life so bliss
I'll handle the worst of you
Because you're the one I love
But please don't make me wait forever
I'm not that tough
Please take care

Of yourself
I can't stand to see you low
It feels like hell
I can't stand to see you
Not feel like yourself
You're normally sunshine
But right you seem unwell
I'll wait for you
For as long as I can
I hope there's a future for us
Where I'm your man
But I don't know
What'll come of us
So I'll just pray
And believe in the power of love

57. The most wonderful girl I know

She's got the warmth of sunshine
She's as cool as a breeze
She'd bring the world to you
If you say please
There's no one like her
There's not a chance
The greatest thing that's happened to me
And with her I want to dance
One smile from her
Mends my tired soul
One touch from her
Makes me feel whole
She's the most
Wonderful girl I know
I thank god I met her
And I hope she knows
How I feel about her
Day in and out
I'm the luckiest man in the universe
She is someone I can't live without
When she's down
It feels like a kick in the face

I can't have her low
I can't have her feel this way
But she is
The strongest person I know
She'll get through this
And after this she'll grow
To someone even more
Fantastic and strong
She'll inspire me to write
Her many more songs
She's the most
Wonderful girl I know
I thank god I met her
And I hope she knows
How I feel about her
Day in and out
I'm the luckiest man in the universe
She is someone I can't live without
She does those little things
That pull at my heart
She's not just an artist
She's a fucking work of art
I see her in my dreams
Everytime I sleep
She's the only one I want
In this life to keep
Close to myself
And attached to my heart
I love you the most

Let's not ever fall apart
She's the most
Wonderful girl I know
I thank god I met her
And I hope she knows
How I feel about her
Day in and out
I'm the luckiest man in the universe
She is someone I can't live without

58. Passenger Princess

I love seeing

You on my passenger seat

Holding my hand

Sitting right next to me

Most of our adventures

Have been dropping you home

Sometimes we go

To a place where we can be alone

And by that I mean my home

When my folks aren't in town

But I want to drive with you

Someplace out of bounds

Where we can be alone

For at least a few days

Forget all our worries

And just melt away

Into the scenery

And experience something new

That's one of the many things

I want with you

We'll drive all around

Wherever the road leads

You're my passenger princess

In this life you're all I need

We'll find someplace cozy
For just you and I
Someplace where we're just
Drinking and looking at the sky
Then we can dance slowly
Under the moonlight
I pull you close to me
And hold you tight
Whisper in your ear
Words I always say
But they'll mean something more
Then they do in the day
I want you everywhere
I want you all the time
I want you forever
Simple cause you're mine
My passenger princess
I'm not dropping you home
You're coming with me
I'm not leaving alone
We're leaving together
And our destination's the same
I want you I need you
This is not a game
My passenger princess
Where shall we go?
You decide the destination
The wheel I'll control
Anyplace where the liquor

Flows like a river
You look like an angel
But you make me feel like a sinner
My passenger princess
You can be the boss of me
Just hold my arm close to you
Use it to rest your cheek
Hold my hand tightly
When I brake hard
You'll always be safe
When I'm driving my car
My passenger princess
You're my favourite person in life
Something about you
Makes me feel alive
You kickstart my heart
And give a shock in my veins
I love you more than
Words can explain

59. Affection

I'm longing for your affection
It's the only thing I need
I'll give you more than
I have ever received
I know you're not yourself
I hate that feeling too
Makes you feel hollow
You don't know what's up with you
Some time for reflection
Will cleanse your mind
It might remind you
That you're divine
I think you're so special
And not just because I'm in love
It's the other way around
I feel god has sent you from above
To find me in this world
So we each have a better half
So we can spend our days together
Cuddling and having a laugh
It's not too much to ask for
If you think about it at all
But for me it's everything
And everything isn't small

I'm craving your affection
It's the thing that I miss
It's more than reassurance
Sometimes it's just a kiss
Sometimes it's holding hands
Sometimes it's a hug
Sometimes it's just a text
Saying I miss you so much
Right now I feel empty
But I know you feel worse
So I'm going to suck it all up
And just end this verse
I love you and want you
To feel like yourself
There's no one better in the world
No one else with whom I've felt
So much love
And so much warmth
So much kindness
Mixed with it all
I'm right here waiting
For you to return
I'll be waiting with affection
For you I yearn

60. Reset

I miss your smile
Your face
Your touch
Your grace
A little bit of you
Is all it takes
To make me happy
To put me in my place
I want your voice
Whispered in my ear
And said out loud
Because I hold you dear
Right in my heart
And deep within my soul
There's no one like you
No one comes close
I want you more
Than you could know
I wish I could reset it all
And then take it slow
I want you, I need you
And I don't want to let go
Let's take one step at a time
Together and we will know

What's next for us
In this life we hold
If it's meant to be
Then together we will grow old
That's what I hope for
And a part of me knows
That you're the one
And it doesn't want to let go
The other part of me
Might not be so sure
But it still wants you
It wants you the most
Everything important in life
Is a leap of faith
It's always scary
You have to give because it takes
Everything from you
And sometimes more
It always wants
What you want to hold
Sometimes I wish
I could turn back time
To fix what went wrong
So you'd always be mine
But what's done is done
It's something we can't change
But there is a future
That's yet to be made
I don't know what it holds

Your guess is as good as mine
But I know it will get better
If we can make it work this time

61. I miss you

I miss our
Night outs together
Those late night drives
In bad weather
After a few drinks
Everything feels better
Holding each other close
So we don't need a sweater
Smoking all our
Worries away
Letting them
Melt just like the day
I dream of this
In my dreams
I dream of what was real
Because it's so serene
The days are not
Kind to me
But I know you have it worse
So I won't speak
I'll just pray
And wish we could be
How we were
And how it should be

I miss you love
That much you know
The depths of this
Is as deep as the snow
In the Antarctic
On a winter night
When there's a blizzard blowing
And nothing's in sight
I seek you in the darkness
Like a guiding light
There's no one quite like you
No one shines that bright
Maybe it's your hair
That's always on fire
You're the reason
For my desire
I miss you
Each and everyday
Every moment without you
Is a moment I wish would go away

62. Goodbye

I'm sorry things didn't turn out
How I had planned in my head
I've always been a dreamer
Even when I'm not in bed
I'm sorry I wasn't able to
Give you what you need
I did what I thought I should
But the situation I didn't read
I'm sorry that I wronged you
When you needed me to be right
I wish I could take it all back
And not be such a blight
I'm sorry I didn't understand
What you needed from me
I was in my own way
And it doesn't fill me with glee
Because I've lost the person
Who meant the world to me
I wish I could fix things
But that's not how it'll be
I walked too many steps
Away from you
I've left you far behind
I wish it wasn't true

But I'm thankful
For loving you
You've made a better man
And I know it's true
I didn't want to lose you
But I guess I did just that
Being away from you
Made me lose track
Of what you needed
To feel like you
But I just wanted you to feel better
Without knowing what's happening with you
I'm sorry for everything
And I hope you can forgive
Me for my indiscretions
I'm sorry for what I did
I still love you
And wished for a better end
But I know it's not possible
So goodbye, this is the end